Neal's Frog

By
M. Loreas

To order additional copies of this book, contact:
Xlibris
1-888-795-4274
www.Xlibris.com
Orders@Xlibris.com

ISBN: Softcover   978-1-4134-9719-9
         Hardcover   978-1-4134-9720-5

Library of Congress Control Number: 2005904779

Print information available on the last page.

Rev. date: 12/13/2019

Dedication
and Acknowledgments

Thank you, God. I dedicate this
book to Neal, Logan, Arthur,
Raymond, Richard, Will and all the
other cute, curious, energetic boys
in the world. Reach inside your
pockets and discover
happy suprises.

So small, on a bamboo tree stem.
The palm of my hand,
I placed him.

And into my pocket, he stayed.
A nice cozy home I made.

Where did I play?
Hmmm..where did I go?
Up the hill, by the pond,
I don't know?

Duane Gillogly

He rolled around as
I rode my bike.
He tumbled, as I ate the cream
I liked.

I jumped and screamed.
Skedaddled and whooped.
In my pocket, he lay cooped.

My final adventure, in the day.
The one not to miss.
At the top of the hill, looked we;
me, and my Big Sis.

The grass a green carpet,
called us to roll on it.

We lay horizontal,
our feet not to touch,
The sun a bright blur,
we giggled so much!

We pushed ourselves forward
into one huge roll.
We screamed the way down
Me, the LOUDEST, I'm told.

Let's do it again! I pleaded;
but a yucky bath was what
I needed.

To the room I go from this
day of bliss.
Tired smile on face, you
couldn't miss.

To peel off clothing
covered with soil.
I pulled off torn sneakers
as part of my toil.

Socks, "peeeuuu"! What a smell!
"Here's a nice warm bath!"
I heard Mom yell.

One last thing to do,
before pants join shoes.
Empty pockets of my collection, too.

Hey ! I pulled out
squished bubble-gum!
Still tasty with sugar,
"mmmm, yum!"

On to the bed post for a
later snack.
I made sure to mark it for
when I came back.

20

Duane Gillogly

Out came the harmonica and
then the kazoo.
The lint, candy wrapper and
rubber band too.

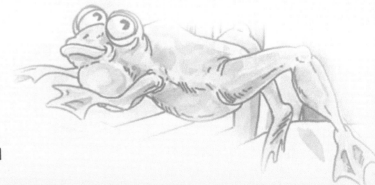

Out came the bottle cap and
my shiny rock.
And out came the frog and
much to my shock!

He was flat as a pancake, more flat;
Much more flat, I say, than that.

I called for Big Sis to have a look.
I was so sad and I couldn't speak.
My day with the frog
ended so bleak.

My frog had gone through the day;
in my pocket, I made him stay.

And now, he was as flat as could be
Wow! His whole day
was spent with me!

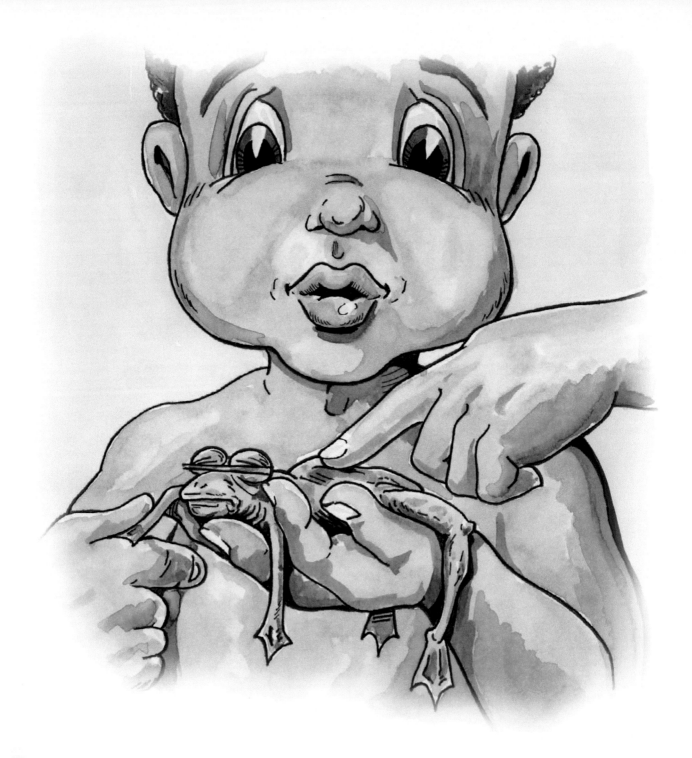

We placed his green body
onto the bed.
And wondered if he was
a little . . . bit . . . . dead.

But as soon as he was clear
of my hand and me,
He SPRANG to life and
jumped free!

Out of the window,
he bounced and popped.
Out of sight,
he jumped and hopped.

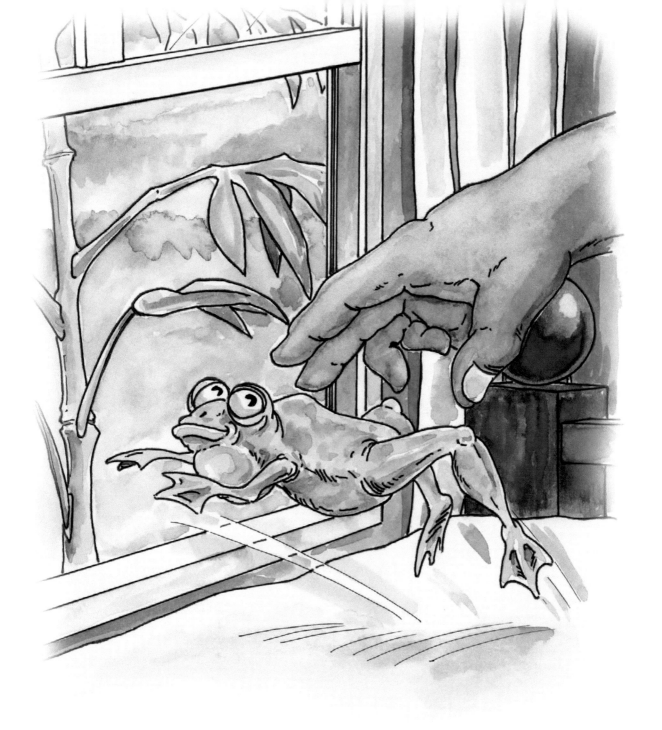

DUANE GILLOGLY

Safely back into his bamboo tree,
where he was first found by me.

The End

Printed in the United States
By Bookmasters